WORLD IN VIEW
ARGENTINA
Nick Caistor

HEINEMANN

HEINEMANN CHILDREN'S REFERENCE
a division of Heinemann Educational Books Ltd
Halley Court, Jordan Hill, Oxford OX2 8EJ

OXFORD LONDON EDINBURGH
MELBOURNE SYDNEY AUCKLAND
MADRID ATHENS BOLOGNA
SINGAPORE IBADAN NAIROBI HARARE
GABORONE KINGSTON PORTSMOUTH NH(USA)

ISBN 0 431 00465 X

British Library Cataloguing in Publication Data
Caistor, Nick
  Argentina
  1. Argentina
  I. Title II. Series
  982'.064

© Heinemann Educational Books Ltd 1990
First published 1990

Designed by Julian Holland Publishing Ltd
Picture research by Jennifer Johnson

Printed in Hong Kong

90 91 92 93 94 95 10 9 8 7 6 5 4 3 2 1

982. 064
8580

Photographic credits: Cover E. Rekos/ZEFA
Title page: Pern/Hutchison Picture Library, 7 Fiona Anderson, 9 Hilary Bradt/South American
Pictures, 10, 12 Hutchison Picture Library, 17 G. Zeisler/Bruce Coleman Ltd, 18 Jan & Des
Bartlett/Bruce Coleman Ltd, 21 Tony Morrison/South American Pictures, 25, 28 Alicia Arendar, 30
Tony Morrison/South American Pictures, 33 Julio Etchart, 36 Popperfoto, 40, 41 Julio Etchart, 44
Alicia Arendar, 47 Tony Morrison/South American Pictures, 48 Moser/Hutchison Picture Library,
51 Tony Morrison/South American Pictures, 53 J Allan Cash, 55 Yorham Lehmann/Robert Harding
Picture Library, 59, 60 Pern/Hutchison Picture Library, 63 Julio Etchart, 65 Robert Harding Picture
Library, 67 Fiona Anderson, 69, 71 Tony Morrison/South American Pictures, 72, 73 Julio Etchart, 74
Tony Morrison/South American Pictures, 77 Industria Argentina, 80, 81, Tony Morrison/South
American Pictures, 83 Sporting Pictures UK, 85, 87, 88 Julio Etchart, 90 Tony Morrison/South
American Pictures, 91 E Rekos/ZEFA, 93 Julio Etchart, 94 Alicia Arendar

Cover: *The Andes, Argentina*
Title page: *Gauchos taking a well-earned rest*

Contents

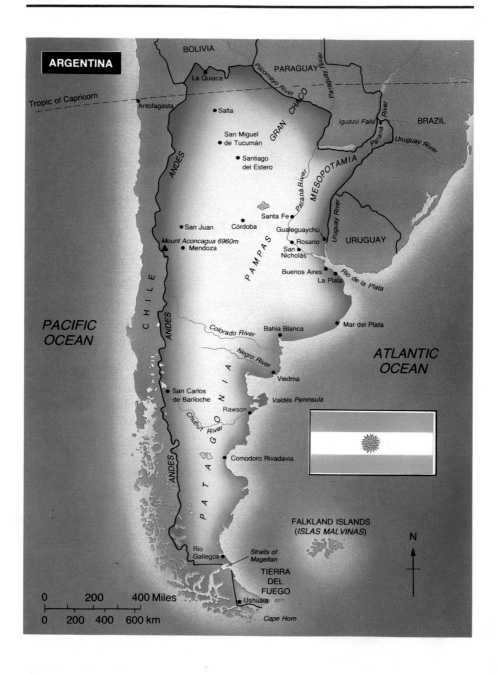

ARGENTINA

BOLIVIA

PARAGUAY

La Quiaca

Tropic of Capricorn

Antofagasta

Pilcomayo River

Paraguay River

GRAN CHACO

Salta

MESOPOTAMIA

Iguazú Falls

BRAZIL

San Miguel
de Tucumán

Santiago
del Estero

Paraná River

Uruguay River

Santa Fe

San Juan   Córdoba

Gualeguaychú

Mount Aconcagua 6960m
Mendoza

Rosario

San
Nicholás

PAMPAS

Buenos Aires

URUGUAY

Uruguay River

Rio de la Plata

La Plata

PACIFIC
OCEAN

CHILE

ANDES

Colorado River

Bahía Blanca

Mar del Plata

Negro River

ATLANTIC
OCEAN

San Carlos
de Bariloche

Viedma

PATAGONIA

Rawson

Valdés Peninsula

Chubut River

Comodoro Rivadavia

ANDES

FALKLAND ISLANDS
(ISLAS MALVINAS)

N

Rio
Gallegos

Straits of
Magellan

TIERRA
DEL
FUEGO

0   200   400 Miles

0   200   400   600 km

Ushuaia

Cape Horn

1 From tropic to pole

The Republic of Argentina is the second largest country in South America, after Brazil. Argentina is 2.8 million square kilometres (over one million square miles) in area, almost a third the size of the United States. Shaped like a triangle, it stretches for 5000 kilometres (3500 miles) down the southeast part of the continent, with its longest side on the west. The western border of Argentina runs from above the Tropic of Capricorn (the furthest point south reached by the sun above the Earth) and tapers to a point at Tierra del Fuego, which is only a few hundred kilometres from the Antarctic.

Like Australia and New Zealand, Argentina occupies the part of the south of the Earth that

Fact Box

Official name	Republic of Argentina
Federal Capital	Buenos Aires
Population (1986 estimate)	31 060 000
Area (sq. km.)	2 780 092 (excluding the disputed Antarctic sector and the Falkland Islands)
Main cities	Córdoba, Rosario, Mendoza, La Plata
Official language	Spanish
Official religion	Roman Catholic
Currency	Austral (= 100 centavos)

Provinces of Argentina

BOLIVIA

PARAGUAY

Tropic of Capricorn

JUJUY

San Salvador de Jujuy

Salta

FORMOSA

Formosa

SALTA

CATAMARCA

San Miguel de Tucumán

CHACO

MISIONES

TUCUMÁN

Resistencia

Corrientes

Posadas

San Fernando de Valle de Catamarca

Santiago del Estero

BRAZIL

SANTIAGO DEL ESTERO

LA RIOJA

CORRIENTES

SANTA FE

La Rioja

SAN JUAN

Córdoba

Santa Fe

San Juan

Paraná

ENTRE RÍOS

URUGUAY

Mendoza

San Luis

CÓRDOBA

MENDOZA

SAN LUIS

Buenos Aires

Santa Rosa

BUENOS AIRES

ATLANTIC OCEAN

LA PAMPA

NEUQUÉN

Neuquén

RÍO NEGRO

PACIFIC OCEAN

CHILE

Viedma

N

Rawson

CHUBUT

SANTA CRUZ

FALKLAND ISLANDS (ISLAS MALVINAS)

Río Gallegos

TIERRA DEL FUEGO

Ushuaia

0   200   400 Miles

0   200   400   600 km

enjoys good rainfall and a climate less extreme than in those countries nearer the Equator. Its seasons are the opposite of those in the northern half of the world, so summer in Argentina is in January and February, and winter in July and August. It is a great distance from Europe and the United States. About 10 000 kilometres (7000 miles) separate Argentina's capital, Buenos Aires, from both New York in North America and London in England.

On the western side of Argentina, the Andes mountains mark the border with Chile. The rivers Pilcomayo, Paraguay, Paraná and Uruguay separate Argentina from Bolivia, Paraguay, Brazil and Uruguay to the north and east.

The Andes mountains

The Andes mountain range is the main feature of western Argentina. The Andes include the highest

The Cerro Cervantes is one of the highest peaks in the Patagonian Andes. The Perito Moreno glacier flows down one side of it into the Lago Argentino. The glacier is three kilometres wide and 50 metres high in some places.

peak in the Americas, Mount Aconcagua (about 7000 metres or 23 000 feet), and several other peaks of over 6000 metres (20 000 feet). In the north, above the Tropic of Capricorn, the Andes mountains are dry and dusty. Near the border with Bolivia they form a high plateau at over 3000 metres (10 000 to 11 000 feet) known as the *puna*. The routes north from Argentina to Bolivia follow the gorges or *quebradas*, which seasonal rivers have cut into this plateau.

Further south, rainfall increases so that the mountain slopes become wooded, while above the timber line the peaks are always white with snow. In the south of Argentina, there are also many mountain lakes and glaciers. Some of the mountains, like Mount Tronador, have become great tourist attractions in the summer months. Tronador means 'The Thunderer', and the mountain has been given this name because of the noise made by giant chunks of ice in its glacier field when the sun melts them.

Tierra del Fuego

Tierra del Fuego is a continuation of the Andes mountains into an island of 21 340 square kilometres (15 000 square miles) off the southern tip of the continent. It was called Tierra del Fuego or 'The Land of Fire' by the early Spanish explorers because they saw the local people's campfires burning on the hills at night. The western side belongs to Chile, the eastern side to Argentina. Tierra del Fuego contains the world's most southerly town at Ushuaia, where the temperature in summer rarely averages more than 10°C (50°F), and falls to 0°C (32°F) in winter.

Ushuaia is the capital and main port of the island of Tierra del Fuego. It is the southernmost town in the world, further south than any places in Australia or New Zealand. In the short summer from December to March, wild flowers bring colour to the dull island landscape.

There is heavy rainfall here all year round, and strong winds usually blow from the Pacific Ocean in the west. The southernmost tip of the island and of the whole continent is Cape Horn, where fierce storms blow for most of the winter months.

Mesopotamia

Argentina's second main geographical region after the Andes is the subtropical area to the east and north of the country which borders on Brazil, Paraguay and Uruguay. It is known as Mesopotamia because it lies between two big rivers, the Uruguay and the Paraná. This reminded the first European settlers in Argentina of the region with the same name in the Middle East, between the rivers Tigris and Euphrates. Here, heavy rainfall, which reaches over 1500

ARGENTINA

The Iguazú River is a tributary of the huge Uruguay River in the north-east of Argentina. At one point on the border with Brazil, there are 275 waterfalls within a kilometre of each other, some of them over 70 metres (230 feet) high.

millimetres (58.5 inches) per year, high temperatures, with an average of almost 30°C (86°F) in the summer months, and flat land produce jungle vegetation in the provinces of Misiones and Corrientes. At one point, the frontier with Brazil is formed by the waterfalls of Iguazú. There are over 270 waterfalls, some of which plunge 70 metres (230 feet). The south of Entre Ríos province is less tropical, and is made up of islands where the Paraná River empties into the

Río de la Plata estuary. These islands consist of mud and sand brought down by the rivers, which make the soil very rich. The islands are often liable to flooding, however.

The Chaco

The Chaco region lies south of the Pilcomayo River on Argentina's northern border with Paraguay, to the west of the Paraná River. This area is part of the Gran Chaco marshland, which extends across southern Paraguay, Brazil and eastern Bolivia. The summer rains flood large areas of this region, while the rest is the kind of subtropical grassland known as savannah. The land rarely rises more than 20 metres (80 feet) above sea-level. It is also very hot. The summer temperature in Formosa, the capital city of Formosa province, which borders on Paraguay, averages 28°C (82°F), and only drops to 18°C (64°F) in the coldest month, July.

The west of the Chaco sees the start of the foothills of the Andes mountain range. The climate here is much drier, and the lush vegetation of the north eastern provinces gives way to scrubland of prickly bushes and cacti, except where river valleys add a touch of green.

The pampas

The vast pampas are Argentina's third region. In Spanish, the word *pampa* means 'level plain', and the pampas are flat grasslands which run for 1500 kilometres (almost 1000 miles) across the centre of the country. They are formed from granite rocks covered by thick deposits of rich, fertile soil brought down from the Andes in rivers over many

The grasslands of central Argentina stretch for hundreds of kilometres. In the north of Argentina they give way to the high deserts of the foothills of the Andes. To the south, they are bordered by the windswept high plateau of Patagonia.

millions of years. In some parts, this fertile soil is nearly 280 metres (1000 feet) deep. In all this expanse, there are almost no hills and very few rivers.

The vegetation of the pampas varies according to how much rain there is. The highest rainfall, and therefore the lushest grass, is in a broad band across the middle of Argentina, known as the *pampa húmeda* or 'wet pampa'. This area is ideal for agriculture and livestock rearing, as temperatures are not too hot; reaching 30°C (86°F) in the summer, and falling only to 12°C (53°F) in the winter months.

Patagonia

The flat land of eastern Argentina gradually rises, and south of the Colorado River, in the province of Río Negro, it is known as Patagonia. The earth is not so fertile as in the wet pampas, except in the valleys of the rivers which flow to the Atlantic. Much of the time, strong winds sweep down from the Andes in the west and the temperature reaches only 12°C (53°F) on average in the summer and is below 0°C (32°F) in May and June. This makes the area cold and unwelcoming, and the vegetation consists mostly of clumps of hardy grass, with few trees. The only exception is in the region's river valleys, where protection from the winds means that grass and trees can thrive. The Atlantic coast of Patagonia is made up of cliffs often 100 metres (over 350 feet) high, as the rocks fall sheer into the water. These cliffs and the high tides mean there are few natural ports along this part of the coastline.

Argentina's greatest river

Most of Argentina's 31 million inhabitants live on the estuary of the huge Río de la Plata (Plate River) on the country's eastern, Atlantic seaboard. The Río de la Plata has an estuary wider than the English Channel, reaching 250 kilometres (180 miles) at its widest point. It separates Argentina to the south from Uruguay on its north bank. In spite of its width, the Río de la Plata is often shallow because of all the soil it carries down. Much of this earth is deposited on the Argentine side of the river, so that the capital, Buenos Aires, has advanced several kilometres into the river since it was first settled by Europeans.

The Atlantic Ocean prevents the temperatures in this part of Argentina from rising as high as they do in the middle of the country, where they can reach well over 40°C (104°F) in the summer. Summer temperatures in Buenos Aires though can reach 35°C (96°F), falling to around 10°C (50°F) in the winter. Cold currents in the Atlantic mean that the sea is never very warm.

Antarctica and the South Atlantic islands

Argentina also claims the part of the continent of Antarctica, which stretches from a few hundred kilometres off the South American mainland as far as the South Pole. Chile and Britain say some of this territory belongs to them, but at the moment there are only isolated scientific research stations

Falklands or Malvinas?

In April 1982, the Argentine armed forces occupied South Georgia and the Falkland Islands, two islands 800 kilometres (500 miles) off the coast of Argentina. Great Britain administers the islands, known to the Argentines as the Islas Malvinas, as a colony. The Argentines claim that the British took the islands from them illegally in 1833 and had always refused to talk about returning them. The British government said that Argentina had never properly occupied the islands, whereas people of British descent had been living there for 150 years under rule from Britain. The two countries fought a war on the islands, which ended in June 1982 with the British regaining control. The new government, which came to power in Argentina in July 1989, finally formally ended the war, and offered to talk about the future of the Falkland Islands. The British government continues to insist that the 2000 people living there must be free to choose which country they are to be governed by.

in these areas. Argentina also lays claim to a number of islands in the South Atlantic, including the Islas Malvinas, or Falkland Islands, which are currently a British colony.

Hummingbirds and great condors

The contrasting regions of Argentina have a varied wildlife, although nowadays it is only in very remote areas that it is plentiful. When the continents drifted apart early in the formation of the Earth, South America was cut off from the rest of the world for millions of years, so that the animal species and plant forms found there developed in ways not found anywhere else in the world.

In the hot jungle areas of north-east Argentina, the tall hardwoods and creepers are home to monkeys, members of the cat family like jaguars and ocelots, wild pigs called peccaries, and ant-eaters. There are as many as 50 kinds of snake, including the coral snake and rattlesnake, and the fer-de-lance, a poisonous snake with beautiful, black diamond shapes all down its back. Tiny, colourful hummingbirds dart among the trees. Their name comes from the noise made by their wings beating as they hover to feed with their long beaks from flowers. Other brightly-coloured birds which live in these trees are the orange-billed toucan and the green parakeet. The rivers of the region of Mesopotamia have many large fish, among the most common being the pejerrey and the surubi.

The Andes regions have very different animals and birds. The best-known bird is the Andean condor, the largest bird of prey in the world. Its wingspan can reach three metres (12 feet) and it uses its wings to glide long distances in the currents of air which rise over the mountains. Condors have been spotted flying 6000 metres (20 000 feet) in the air. The rocks of the mountains are ideal for the vicuña and the guanaco, the long-legged Andean deer similar to the llama. Their natural hunters are the mountain cats and the pumas which are still numerous in the remoter parts of the Andes. In the southern part of the Andes region, there are large forests of beech and pine. There are also many araucaria or monkey puzzle trees, some of which live over 1000 years. Wild cats and foxes thrive in these forests, and campers are occasionally woken by a curious bear. A very different sight in the southern mountain

---

Darwin and the voyage of HMS Beagle

The English naturalist Charles Darwin visited Argentina as a young man between 1832 and 1834. He was sailing round the world on the HMS *Beagle*, which was making scientific studies of nature in many different regions. In the diary he kept of this voyage, Darwin wrote an account of all the animals and plant species he saw. He was interested in how they were different but similar in each continent because they had adapted to suit the conditions in which they found themselves. What he observed during his trip later led him to think that animals, including man, had evolved or developed gradually from earlier ancestors. When he set out his theory of evolution in his book *The Origin of Species* it caused a great scandal, as many religious people believed that God had created man from nothing.

The Andean condor is the largest bird of prey in the world. It lives high up, and feeds mostly on dead meat. Its wonderful eyesight enables it to spot its food while soaring high above the mountains.

province of Santa Cruz is a petrified forest of trees which have become fossils, some of them 30 metres (100 feet) long and one metre (just over three feet) round. The fossilized trees have been calculated as being 70 million years old.

Wildlife of the pampas and the coast

The pampas are a paradise for birds. The flat marshes are ideal for many thousands of coots, plovers, flamingoes and cranes. The fences and telegraph poles of the pampas are used by the oven bird, or *hornero*, so called because it makes a clay nest shaped like a beehive oven on the poles. The strangest of all the birds of the pampas is the American ostrich, the *ñandu* or rhea, which is about 1.5 metres (five feet) high, but cannot fly despite having wings. The cowboys or *gauchos* of the pampas used to hunt these birds by throwing leather balls to wrap round their legs and bring them to the ground, but nowadays the ñandu are a protected species.

The grasslands are also home to armadillos, brown, sharp-nosed creatures with a specially tough skin on their backs. When attacked they roll into a ball like a hedgehog. Most of the animals on the pampas are rodents, creatures which live in holes, and feed on grass, insects and other small animals. Common among these are the vizcacha, a small rodent hunted for its fur, and the *mara* or Patagonian hare.

The pampas did not have many trees apart from the ombu – but many poplars and eucalyptus have been planted in the past hundred years. They are always a welcome sight on these flat lands, because it means that there is water nearby, and possibly a ranch or a village.

The Atlantic coast of Argentina is also rich in animal life. Penguins and sea lions breed on the

The ombu tree

W H Hudson was a writer whose family went to Argentina from the United States in the 1830s. In his old age, he recalled his childhood on the pampas in a book called *Far Away and Long Ago*. Here is his description of the typical pampas tree, the ombu:

'The ombu is a very singular tree indeed ... and has an immense girth – 40 or 50 feet in some cases; at the same time the wood is so soft and spongy that it can be cut into with a knife, and is utterly unfit for firewood, for when cut up it refuses to dry, but simply rots away like a ripe water-melon. It also grows slowly, and its leaves, which are large, glossy, and deep green, like laurel leaves, are poisonous.'

Valdés peninsula, about 800 kilometres (500 miles) south of the capital Buenos Aires. The Valdés peninsula is one of the most interesting areas for wildlife in all Argentina. There are whale breeding grounds in the seas off southern Argentina where species like the Southern Right whale go to have their young. Further south, Blue whales, the largest animals in the world, can still occasionally be found.

2   Argentina's past

Cave paintings and other remains found in the south of Argentina suggest that the first people lived there about 12 000 years ago. Experts still argue whether these people arrived in Argentina from further north on the American continent, or if they crossed the Pacific Ocean in boats from the Polynesian islands and colonized Chile and Argentina. The earliest Argentines hunted wild animals and collected fruit and seeds to eat. They lived in small groups and did not make permanent homes, but often lived in caves or other natural shelters. The Los Toldos cavern in the southern province of Santa Cruz has many beautiful paintings of hands and animals, and is thought to have been lived in about 11 000 years ago. On the Atlantic coast in Patagonia and Tierra del Fuego, the early inhabitants lived off the sea. Archaeologists explored one site on the southern coast of Tierra del Fuego that was found to contain many shells and the bones of sea animals which had been shaped into tools.

Altogether, about a hundred local tribes lived in different parts of Argentina. They seem to have had little contact with each other or with the world beyond, and did not produce any of the developed civilizations found further north on the continent. It was in the north of Argentina that these people began to settle and live by farming rather than hunting. Between about 500BC and AD600 the inhabitants of what are now the provinces of Jujuy, San Juan and Tucumán apparently began to grind corn, to make pottery and to produce

The people who lived in Tucumán and other areas of northern Argentina made stone statues of their gods. Some of them are three metres (over nine feet) high, and show stylised human features or patterns. None of the beliefs of these people are still held today.

stone sculptures. In the Tafi valleys of Tucumán some of these stones have carved human features. These people built their houses grouped around a patio or central courtyard. Their food seems to have been mostly cereals, potatoes and maize. They kept llamas for their wool and meat.

These scattered cultures did not go through any great changes in the next thousand years. In some areas, their pottery became more elaborate, in others, metal objects were made. Their houses were still very simple, and there were no large settlements that could be called towns. They have left behind pots, weapons, and evidence that they used looms to produce cloth, but no written history of their way of life in Argentina before the Spaniards came.

In 1480, the Incas, who had a strong empire in Peru and Bolivia, conquered the people living in the northern Argentine Andes mountains. They organized the local groups as part of their kingdom. The fortified places they built, called *pucara*, their pottery and other remains can be seen today. They also constructed a road, known as the Route of the Incas, which covered 1000 kilometres (600 miles) down from Bolivia to Mendoza in the west of Argentina. When the Spaniards arrived in the sixteenth century, they estimated that there were as many as 300 000 indigenous people living in what is now called Argentina, mostly in the foothills of the northern Andes.

The Spaniards arrive

The first Europeans to explore Argentina were the Spaniards and the Portuguese. A Spanish explorer, Juan Díaz de Solis sailed into the estuary of the Río de la Plata in 1516. He and nearly all his men were killed by local tribesmen. The next European to sail up the estuary, in 1526, was the explorer Sebastian Cabot. He gave the estuary the name 'Río de la Plata', which in Spanish means 'river of silver'. Like many European explorers, Cabot thought the river must lead to kingdoms in Latin America with treasures of silver, like those that had been found in Mexico and Peru. The Portuguese explorer Fernando de Magellan sailed down Argentina's Atlantic coast in 1520 on his voyage round the world. He crossed into the Pacific through the straits between the mainland and Tierra del Fuego. These straits were named the Straits of Magellan in his honour.

Other Spaniards came down across the Andes from their settlements in Peru, and founded cities in the north of Argentina. A Spanish nobleman named Pedro de Mendoza first founded what he called 'Santa María de los Buenos Aires' on 3 February 1536. After a short while, he and his followers were forced to abandon the new settlement. It was only in 1580 that Buenos Aires was successfully established by the Spaniards. The oldest continuously lived-in town in Argentina is Santiago del Estero in the north-west, which was created in 1551. Still more Spanish explorers crossed from Chile on the Pacific side of the Andes mountains and set up the town of Mendoza in western Argentina.

The Spaniards fought with the local people, and

Missionaries

In the eighteenth century, Jesuit missionaries from Spain brought Christianity to the Guaraní Indians in the north-east of Argentina. They settled the nomadic people in villages, where they built fine churches and other buildings. The villagers planted crops and shared all they earned among the community. In 1767, the Jesuits were expelled from Argentina. The King of Spain, Carlos III, was frightened that the Jesuits were becoming too powerful, and ordered that they should no longer be allowed to work anywhere in the Spanish empire. The Guaraní Indians were sent away from the villages again, and the Jesuit settlements fell into ruin. The ruined sites can still be visited in the Argentine province of Misiones, and the story of these settlements was told in the recent feature film *The Mission*.

drove them off their lands, though much of the pampas and Patagonia were still controlled by the original inhabitants. The Spaniards were Christians and converted as many of the tribes as possible to Christianity. They brought cattle and horses with them, and Argentina's economy was based on these animals for the next 250 years since it did not have the mineral riches of the other Spanish colonies.

The Spanish king only allowed the colonies to trade with Spain, and all this commerce had to take place through ports in Mexico and Peru. This meant that Argentina, a long way from both these centres, was very isolated. Buenos Aires did not grow as a port, although it was on the Atlantic coast facing Europe.

The towns in the interior of Argentina were more important. Agricultural produce, horses and mules were sent from Argentina north to Peru. The cattle brought by the Spaniards escaped and increased in numbers in the ideal conditions of the pampas. The local cowboys or gauchos lived off these cattle, hunting them down and selling their meat, hides and fat to people in the towns.

As the Spanish settlers inter-married with the local people, a mixed race of Argentines grew up, especially in the countryside. In the towns, the Spaniards tended to marry with others of similar background, creating a group of people called *criollos* who had Spanish blood although they had been born in Argentina. In the eighteenth century, there were perhaps 250 000 to 500 000 of these two groups of Argentines, about the same number of local people, and as many as 80 000 black people, most of them slaves or former slaves.

The cabildo *or council building in Buenos Aires. This is where the Spanish administration used to meet to discuss how to run the colony of Argentina in the eighteenth century. In 1808, the people of Buenos Aires held their own meetings there at the start of their revolt against rule by the Spaniards.*

Independence

It was not until 1776 that Argentina became a centre of the Spanish empire. In that year it was made into a vice-royalty, which meant that political and commercial decisions could be made in Buenos Aires rather than in Peru. Buenos Aires could also trade directly with Spain, and at once grew in size and importance. A survey in 1780 put the population of Buenos Aires at 35 000. Shortly afterwards, the first printing press, the first hospitals, and a theatre were set up there. The Argentines in Buenos Aires and other towns

The Afro-Argentines
In the late eighteenth century, almost 17 per cent of Argentina's non-native population were Africans or their descendants. Black slaves had been brought into the country by their Spanish owners since the first days of settlement in the sixteenth century. They were mostly employed as domestics or labourers in the towns. By the end of the nineteenth century, however, Afro-Argentines made up only one per cent of the people. It seems that many died in the armies during the fight for independence at the start of the nineteenth century, since one way slaves could win their freedom was by volunteering to fight against the Spaniards. By 1827, most of the black slaves had been granted their freedom, but records of them as a group in the Argentine population disappear by the mid-1800s. Some people think that the rhythm of African drum music can be heard in the music of the Argentine dance, the tango.

wanted to be able to buy and sell goods where they liked. They were also tired of being a colony of Spain, and having to pay taxes to that country.

The war of independence by Britain's colonies in North America, from 1775 to 1776, and the ideas of freedom which inspired the French revolution in 1789, made the people in Argentina and the other Spanish colonies in Latin America want to become independent from Spain. These feelings were strengthened when the British navy, under Admiral Lord Nelson, destroyed the Spanish fleet at the battle of Trafalgar in 1805. This meant the Spaniards could no longer protect Argentina in any way. In 1806, a force of British soldiers invaded Buenos Aires. When they were defeated by local rather than Spanish troops, this too increased the pressure for Argentina to declare itself an independent country.

It was Napoleon's invasion of Spain in 1808 that gave those Argentines who wanted independence their chance. They set up their own town council in Buenos Aires, and forced the Spanish governor to resign. On 25 May 1810, an independent government was set up in Buenos Aires. This day is now celebrated as marking Argentina's independence, though battles with troops loyal to Spain continued for another six years. The links with Spain were not formally broken until 9 July 1816 in the town of Tucumán.

Argentina's hero

One of the most successful Argentine generals in the war against the Spaniards was José de San Martín. He had fought with the Spanish troops against the French in Spain before returning to Argentina in 1812 to fight for its independence. When this had been secured, he gathered a large army of Argentines and crossed the Andes mountains near Mendoza to help the Chileans in their struggle for freedom. Together, they defeated the Spanish army in 1817 and 1818, and Chile was freed from Spanish rule. San Martín then used ships to carry his army to Lima in order to help drive the Spaniards from Peru. However, on his return to Buenos Aires in 1823, General San Martín found there was no place for him in the politics of the new country. He left for France, and died in exile in Boulogne in 1852. It was only after his death that he began to be considered

Argentina's greatest hero, and now nearly every town has his statue or a street named after him.

Caudillos

Though Argentina was now free from Spain, the new country was not yet unified. The provinces in the north wanted to be separate from Buenos Aires. The territories on the north side of the Río de la Plata broke away to form another country, Uruguay. For the first 20 years of its new life in the nineteenth century, power in Argentina passed backwards and forwards between the forces supporting rule by the provinces and those who backed Buenos Aires.

From 1828 to 1852, Argentina was ruled by the dictator Manuel Rosas, a *caudillo* or provincial leader with a strong personal following. He brought in a reign of terror in which many of his opponents were murdered, and Argentina was often torn by fighting. Rosas was overthrown in 1852 by General Urquiza, and in 1853 a national constitution was drawn up which is still Argentina's basic set of laws. At the time, however, the people in Buenos Aires refused to recognize General Urquiza as their president, and set up as a country on their own. It was only in 1862 that Buenos Aires and the other provinces were finally brought together again, and Argentina became a unified territory. Three more provinces: Chaco, Formosa and Misiones, were added to the country as a result of victory in a long and bloody war against Paraguay from 1865 to 1870.

The Republic

From 1862, Argentina was a republic headed by a president and with laws passed by a parliament. The presidents Bartolomé Mitre (1862-1868), Domingo Faustino Sarmiento (1868-1874) and Nicolás Avellaneda (1874-1880) helped strengthen government according to the constitution. These three presidents created the modern Argentina. They unified the country by defining provincial boundaries, setting up a national army, encouraging railways and other communication systems, and setting up a central administration. Public health and education were also introduced and structured. In 1884, a law made public education non-religious, and the universities all became state-run. Mitre, Sarmiento and Avellaneda looked towards Europe as 'civilization', and encouraged trade and other links with that continent rather than with the rest of Latin America.

In the 1870s, a campaign to gain proper control of all the land of Argentina was carried out. In what was known as the 'war of the desert' most of the Araucanian Indians who still lived in great areas of the pampas were killed or driven off the rich grasslands.

At that time, Britain was the world's leading sea power. Much of Argentina's beef, leather, mutton and wool was shipped there, while in return the British sold their manufactured goods in Argentina. The British also built Argentina's railway system, with Buenos Aires as its centre, so that meat exports could be brought to the port more rapidly. This period at the end of the

Argentina has been a major meat-producing nation for many years. At first the cowboys or gauchos made their homes wherever they pleased on the pampas, killing the wild cattle and selling the meat and hides. Nowadays, all the gauchos work and live on big ranches or estancias. *Their clothes and work have changed very little since the nineteenth century.*

nineteenth century was one of great expansion and prosperity in Argentina. By the beginning of this century, it was the richest nation in Latin America. Much of this wealth was based on agriculture. The number of cattle in Argentina doubled between 1880 and 1900, and land used for growing crops increased ten times.

The new Argentines

This expansion encouraged the Argentine government to invite immigrants from Europe to come to live in Argentina. Between 1880 and 1900, over one million Europeans went to live there, and this wave of immigration continued until the 1950s. In the early years of the twentieth century, Argentina was second only to the United States in the number of European newcomers settling there. Many came from Italy and Spain, believing that America would be a place free from poverty, hardship or political problems. Thousands of Jewish people emigrated to Argentina from Russia and Poland, as did Arabs from Syria and Lebanon. British people went out to look after the railways, the trams, the banks, and many agricultural estates, and Argentina had the largest British colony outside the countries of the British Empire.

Buenos Aires became a great international city with an exciting intellectual and political life, for the newcomers brought European ideas and traditions. The immigrants started some of the first factories producing textiles, footwear and building materials. They also opened many new shops selling the specialities of their former countries.

The First World War from 1914 to 1918 only

helped make Argentina richer, as its exports of food were needed all the more in the countries of Europe fighting the war. After 1916, the new Radical party, which was supported by the immigrants and people who lived in the cities and towns, won political power from the landowners and the military. By the 1920s, the people were growing more and more unhappy with the government, especially when Argentina's economic situation grew much worse with the 1929 worldwide economic crisis, known as the Depression, when most businesses collapsed and many people had no work. In 1930, the armed forces rebelled against the government and took power.

3 Perón and other generals

Since 1930, Argentina has only had short periods of properly elected civilian government, and many years of rule by the military and their supporters. In 1989, the Radical party's Raúl Alfonsín became the first civilian president in 50 years to hand over

The Congreso or parliament building is in the centre of Buenos Aires. The Senate and the House of Representatives meet here regularly to discuss and pass laws on all aspects of life in Argentina. The square in front of the Congreso building is the start of measurements for all road distances in Argentina.

peacefully to another elected president. From 1930 to 1943, military governments and corrupt civilians took turns in power. They ruled mostly by corruption and force. Even when politicians with views opposing theirs had a majority in the Congress or national parliament, their decisions were never respected. The governments of this period saw Argentina above all as a country which should produce and export meat and cereals from its agricultural heartlands and live on the money produced by this trade. There were fewer new immigrants from Europe in those years, and the attempts of those workers already in Argentina to organize in trade unions were resisted by force.

The military and the landowners

Most of the land was owned by a few rich people, so many of the poorer agricultural workers who lived in the interior of Argentina came to Buenos Aires and the other cities of the eastern seaboard to look for work. They joined the immigrants who had come at the beginning of the century and now had children, and became part of a whole new group of town-living workers. The economic problems of the countries which usually supplied Argentina with goods meant they no longer sent them. New factories were opened and Argentina began to produce more goods of its own, despite little encouragement from its own government. The military rulers and their wealthy landowning friends did very little to help these people working in the new factories or in the traditional industries. Someone was soon to come on the scene who would recognize that they were now one of the most powerful groups in Argentina.

The Perón years

In 1943, among a group of young officers who seized power was the young colonel Juan Domingo Perón. He became the minister for Labour and Social Welfare, and used this position to build up support among the workers. He helped form trade unions, and brought in paid holidays, minimum wages and social security payments. This made him the champion of the working people, but immediately led the employers, the landowners and the traditional politicians to become very suspicious of him. In 1945, his military colleagues threw him out of the government and put him in jail. Perón's working-class supporters took over Buenos Aires and a week later he was set free and returned to the government.

When a presidential election was held in 1946, Perón was the easy winner. He was to be president for the next nine years. Argentina was then enjoying another rich period, mainly because it supplied food to hungry European countries after the Second World War which ended in 1945. The war also meant that Argentine industries had to make their own goods instead of importing them, so local industry continued to grow. Perón encouraged this by protecting products made in Argentina and offering cheap loans to Argentine industrialists. His government also nationalized many industries, bringing them under the control of the state. In 1948 for example, the Argentine government bought the railway system from its British owners, at the cost of one year's meat exports to Britain.

Perón married his second wife, Eva, in 1946.

Eva Perón was the first woman to be in the forefront of Argentine politics. At the end of the 1940s she was even more popular than her husband, President Perón, especially among women and the poor people in the interior of Argentina.

Together they used some of the wealth Argentina enjoyed in the second half of the 1940s to help the poorer people in Argentine society. These people followed them in the Peronist movement and idolized Evita, as she was known. It was thanks to her that Argentine women were given the right to vote in 1949. Perón however was a modern caudillo, a strong leader who wanted to rule in his own way and did not like any opposition. A majority of people supported him at first, but he also made many enemies. Although he was re-elected as president in 1951, Argentina was

Evita Perón (whose real name was Maria Eva Duarte de Perón) was the idol of many poor Argentines in the late 1940s and early 1950s. She met Colonel Juan Domingo Perón in 1944, and married him in 1946. By collecting money to build hundreds of hospitals, schools and clinics she won the loyalty of his supporters. The poor labourers who worked with their shirts off and were known as the *descamisados* (shirtless ones) were particularly devoted to her. Her rise from being an unknown actress to become the wife of the president seemed like a fairy tale to many Argentines. She died of cancer in 1952 at the age of 33. She was such a powerful symbol that the military who overthrew President Perón stole Evita's body and had it sent secretly to Europe. It was only after her husband's death in 1974 that her body was returned to Argentina. The inscription on her tomb reads: 'Don't cry for me, Argentina, I remain quite near you.'

beginning to have problems. Its exports were not earning as much money as in previous years, and Argentine industry could not produce enough goods. Prices began to rise rapidly, and wages increased quickly too. The country began to experience inflation, which has been one of its biggest problems ever since. Although Perón's working-class supporters were earning more money, it was not enough to buy them as much food or as many goods as in the early years of his rule. Eva Perón died in 1952, and with her death Perón lost a valuable organizer and popular leader.

All this cost Perón a lot of support. Many politicians, intellectuals, and other leading people in Argentina were against his attempts to limit freedom of speech and ideas. His government closed down newspapers and magazines which criticized Peronism. Opposition politicians were often jailed or forced to live abroad. Schools and universities were closely controlled, and taught obedience to Peronism. The Catholic Church also opposed Perón because some priests had been arrested and gangs of his supporters had burnt churches. His government also tried to abolish Catholic schools and introduce divorce. In 1955, with the backing of all these opponents, the armed forces removed General Perón from power.

Exile and return

Perón lived in exile for the next 18 years, in various Latin American countries and finally in Spain. Despite this, his personality and his political movement remained very important for many people in Argentina. The civilian governments during the rest of the 1950s and 1960s found it impossible to govern without the support of the trade unions, who were still loyal to Perón. When the armed forces took over government, they found it even harder to work out a proper plan for progress. Eventually, in 1973, the military President General Lanusse decided to call elections in which the Peronist party would be allowed to stand again as a political party.

The violent seventies

The Peronist party won these elections, and General Perón returned to Argentina as president in 1973. Two million people went to greet him, but the fierce shooting between different groups of his own supporters was a warning of the violence to come. By now Perón was 76, and in poor health. He died a year later, without ever getting to grips with the country's problems. His third wife, Isabel, became president, but the Peronist movement was split into many groups, who could not agree on what to do. Once again, the armed forces stepped in, and in 1976 forced Isabel Perón to resign. General Videla of the army got together with the navy and airforce leaders to form what they called a 'government of national reconstruction'. They stopped all political and trade union activity, and governed by issuing decrees which were not allowed to be questioned. They were determined to put an end to revolutionary Peronism. To do this they took over the radio and television and controlled all the news in newspapers and magazines. They brought schools and universities under military control to make sure students were not being taught 'revolutionary' ideas. Many thousands of Argentines were forced to move abroad because of their political beliefs. The armed forces' government, or *junta*, put many politicians and trade unionists into jail. Worse still, they fought what became known as a 'dirty war' to get rid of people they saw as their opponents. These included not only the revolutionary Peronist groups, but anyone else who spoke out against them. Between 1976 and 1982, at least 9000 Argentines 'disappeared' and were never seen or heard of again after being captured by members of the police or armed forces. Nearly all of them were tortured and then killed without any trial or even admission by the authorities that they were

Each day the families and mothers of those who had 'disappeared' during the military regime of the late 1970s, walk silently round the Plaza de Mayo square in front of the presidential palace. They are protesting that the authorities have given no news of their children, who were never seen alive again. They wear a white headscarf as a symbol of their protest.

holding these people prisoner. The armed forces thought this was the best way to root out opposition to its ideas and policies, and got rid of opponents despite many protests inside Argentina and abroad.

War and defeat for the military

These policies and the many other restrictions on normal life soon led the Argentines to reject military rule. President Galtieri, who took over in 1980, decided that a good way to win more support for the military government would be to show the Argentines that the armed forces could win a spectacular victory. For many years, the Argentines have said that the Falkland Islands (Islas Malvinas) belong to them and that the British have no right to be there. So at the start of April 1982, Galtieri sent Argentine troops to take over the islands. Two months later, British troops

Argentines frequently demonstrate in the street over political questions. Here a huge crowd has gathered in the Plaza de Mayo square to support the civilian president Raul Alfonsín against the danger of a takover of power by the armed forces.

41

won the islands back, and this helped to bring about the fall of the military government in Argentina. At the end of 1983, elections were held for a civilian government. The leader of the Radical party, Raúl Alfonsín, was chosen as president, ending eight years of military rule.

For the next six years, President Alfonsín tried to bring Argentina back to normal political and social life. All political and trade union activities were allowed again, and nearly all the political prisoners were set free. The newspapers, television and radio could mention everything completely freely. Many of the exiles who had gone to live abroad returned immediately, and there was a new sense of hope and creativity in the world of literature, cinema and the other arts. President Alfonsín also set up a commission to investigate the deaths of civilians that had taken place under the military government. Several of the junta leaders were convicted of crimes against human rights and put in prison. However, a military revolt which almost toppled Alfonsín from power persuaded him not to bring any more officers to trial. This lost him a lot of support from ordinary Argentines who wanted to see their former military rulers punished. Nor could President Alfonsín find a way to bring the Argentine economy under control. His government tried to stop inflation by not allowing either wages or prices to increase. It also introduced a new currency, the *austral*, which at first was equal in value to the United States dollar. This plan worked for a while, but then once again prices began to rise very quickly, and his government became even more unpopular.

Currency and inflation
For many years, the Argentine currency was the peso. But inflation meant that each peso was worth less and less, and the Argentine central bank had to print new money all the time. In July 1985, the Alfonsín government introduced a new unit of currency, the austral. At the beginning one austral was equal to one thousand of the old pesos, and was worth almost one US dollar. But by the middle of 1989, one US dollar could buy 700 australes. A letter sent to England from Argentina in January 1989 cost nine australes. One sent in March cost 18, one in May 120 australes, and another in July cost 350 australes. By June 1990 there were 5000 australes to the US dollar. This makes it very hard for the government, businessmen, shopkeepers and families to calculate how much they will need to spend or save.

The return of the Peronists

New elections were held in May 1989. President Alfonsín fulfilled his promise to keep the country under democratic civilian government but, to many people's surprise, it was the other main party, the Peronists, that won these elections. The Peronist candidate Carlos Menem became president in July 1989, with Argentina facing yet another economic crisis.

The Peronist government of Carlos Menem faces many challenges. It has to find new ideas and policies for government that will unite Argentina, rather than divide it as the Peronists have done in the past. It has to find a way to change now that its leader, General Perón, is dead, and a way to find solutions that will help Argentina in the 1990s.

The 1989 elections took place without any violence, and it seemed that the vast majority of Argentines were keen to continue with a civilian government. What they most wanted to avoid was any return to rule by the armed forces, which had threatened many of their rights as individuals and as citizens.

The Casa Rosada or 'pink house' is the president's government house in Buenos Aires. Built in 1894, it is always painted in a distinctive pink colour, although nobody is quite sure why. In front of it is the Plaza de Mayo square, with a monument commemorating May 1810 when Argentina first declared itself independent from Spain.

The Argentine state

Argentina is a representative federal republic. According to the 1853 constitution (amended in 1880) Argentina consists of 22 provinces and the national territory of Tierra del Fuego, Antarctica and the South Atlantic islands. The city of Buenos Aires is the federal capital, in the way that Washington DC is the capital of the United States. Each province has its own parliament, consisting

of a Chamber of Deputies and a Senate. The federal parliament is based in the Congreso building in Buenos Aires. The political representatives in the Chamber of Deputies are elected by the votes of all men and women over 18. Voting is compulsory. There is also a Senate, made up of two members from each province, chosen by the provincial parliaments.

The main political parties are: the Justicialist party (The Peronists), The Radical Civic Union (The Radical party), the Democratic Centre Union, and the Intransigent party. The Justicialist party's supporters come mainly from the workers in the towns and the provinces. The party follows the ideas of General Perón, but is looking for ways to make the movement meet the challenges of the 1990s.

The Radical Civic Union (the Radical party) was founded in 1890, and after enjoying power from 1916 to 1930 found itself overtaken by the Peronists until Raúl Alfonsín was successful in the 1983 elections. It is closely linked to social democratic ideas, believing in gradually improving society. Its supporters have traditionally been townspeople with office jobs for the government or state-run industries.

The Democratic Centre Union is a conservative, right-wing party, which supports the big landowners and business interests.

The Intransigent party is a moderate left-wing party which enjoys support among intellectuals and students, but has not won the mass backing that the Peronists have achieved.

4 Aberdeen Angus and sunflowers

One in six Argentines works directly in agriculture. Although Argentina is known mostly as a producer and exporter of beef, large areas of the pampas are used for growing cereals and other crops. Argentina is also the world's fifth largest producer of wine, while in Patagonia there are over 35 million sheep.

Cattle on the pampas
Cattle have been raised on the fertile pampas since the time the Spaniards first explored Argentina. With plenty of water and grass, the conditions were ideal for cattle, and their numbers increased very quickly. For many years the cattle were simply killed for their leather or fat, and the meat was thrown away because it was impossible to keep it fresh for long enough to sell it. At the beginning of the nineteenth century, the idea of salting meat to help preserve it meant that more beef could be sold. It was only about a hundred years ago that Argentina began to export the carcasses, thanks to new ways of freezing the meat in ships that could carry it to Europe where it could be sold as fresh meat.

The British built railways to help transport the cattle alive to the ports, so that they could be slaughtered immediately before the export of the carcasses. The British also introduced better kinds of grass to the pampas, and brought over new breeds of cattle like the Shorthorns and the

Herds of cows graze all year round on the pampas. They provide mostly beef, though there are large herds of milk cows closer to the big cities.

Aberdeen Angus. These breeds produced the type of beef that Europeans liked best. The increasing population of Argentina meant that more people at home wanted to buy beef, and this kind of agriculture has boomed since the last years of the 1800s. Most cattle are raised on *estancias* or large estates which have herds of many thousands. The climate is so good that the cattle never need to be brought inside or be given any food apart from the grass they can find for themselves.

Today, cattle and beef continue to be a major part of Argentina's agriculture. Britain is the biggest buyer of Argentina's famous corned beef, which is made by boiling salt beef at a high temperature. Argentina also sells a lot of meat to Italy and the Soviet Union. The cattle are rounded up once a year, and sent by road or railway to

Buenos Aires or one of the other ports on the Río de la Plata. There, the animals are killed in large *mataderos* or slaughterhouses, and the meat sent to be frozen while waiting for shipment abroad. The Argentines themselves eat a large amount of their own beef (an average of 100 kilos or over 220 pounds a year) and frequently have steak twice a day. Governments have tried to encourage them to eat something different, so that the country can export more meat and earn more foreign money, but Argentine eating habits are hard to change.

Merino sheep are the favourite type all over Patagonia in southern Argentina. Their thick wool protects them from the strong westerly winds that sweep down from the Andes. They are sheared in November, at the end of the Argentine spring.

Sheep in Patagonia

Argentines only occasionally eat another of the country's main agricultural products, meat from Argentina's sheep, lamb and mutton. Almost all this meat is exported. Over the past hundred years, sheep farming has been pushed out of the

best lands in the pampas because more money was to be made from cattle or cereals. Now sheep are farmed almost entirely in Patagonia. The grass there is not so lush and the weather conditions not so good as in the central pampas region, but the hardy breeds of sheep like Merino and Australian are able to cope. The size of the farms is very large by European standards, with sheep being allowed to graze freely over thousands of square kilometres. A large number of the farms are owned or managed by British people who settled here in the nineteenth century. The sheep are sheared at the end of spring in November, and their wool sent either up to Buenos Aires and the other centres of population, or exported directly. Lamb and mutton are also exported from Patagonia and Tierra del Fuego.

Cereals on the pampas
The growing of cereals and oil-producing plants is also very widespread on the fertile soil of the pampas. Wheat has been grown in the provinces of Buenos Aires and Santa Fé since the end of the last century, when the Argentine government allowed the immigrants from Europe to rent or to buy land. Italians, Spaniards and others began to produce wheat to make bread (which had been a luxury until then). As Argentina is in the southern half of the world, it is summer there when it is winter in Europe and the United States. Over a long period of time during the early years of the twentieth century, therefore, thousands of poor Spaniards and Italians would go to Argentina to work in the wheat harvest, and then return to their home countries for the harvest in Europe. They

were known as *golondrinas* or swallows, because they came and went with the summer. Nowadays, machines have replaced many of the workers; the flat lands and large fields making it easy for tractors and harvesters to operate quickly and effectively. Jeeps and cars have also taken over from the gaucho's horses, but there are still an estimated 2.5 million horses in Argentina.

As well as wheat, maize is grown in many parts of the north-eastern pampas, where the weather is hotter. It is also grown by the people who live in the Andes, for whom it has always been the staple food. The maize is harvested in autumn and used for flour, oil starch and for animal feed. Other cereals grown in lesser amounts include oats and barley, used mostly for Argentina's large beer industry.

In recent years, much land has been used for

Forestry

Argentina has a large amount of forest land, recently estimated at 60 000 square kilometres (23 000 square miles). Two thirds of the trees are said to be of wood that could be used by man, but the timber industry has never been well planned or controlled. In some areas like the Chaco, trees such as the *quebracho* were felled without thought, for use as railway sleepers or for extracting tannin for the leather industry. This left huge areas of the jungle without trees, and damaged the whole countryside. In recent years, some softwoods like pine and poplar have been planted, especially in the Andes, and these are being used systematically to produce cellulose for making paper.

oil-bearing plants. Linseed is grown on higher ground and used in the paint industry as well as for making a cake for feeding cattle. Sunflowers, which the Spaniards originally discovered on the Great Plains of North America, are grown in the pampas round Buenos Aires where huge fields of the yellow flowers make a spectacular sight. There has also been a rapid expansion in the production of crops of soya beans and sorghum, which also grow well in the pampas and produce oil for export.

Sugar, tropical fruit and other crops

In the north of Argentina, which is too hot for cattle or cereals, tropical fruit and sugar are grown. It was the Spanish Jesuits who introduced sugar-cane to San Miguel de Tucumán, in the

Two thirds of Argentina's sugar is grown in the northern province of Tucumán. Harvesting is still done mostly by hand, and provides a few weeks' work for thousands of labourers who otherwise have few jobs.

centre of Argentina about 1400 kilometres north-west of Buenos Aires. Today, many people from the northern mountain areas are employed for a few months each year to do the cutting of the cane on big estates or *ingenios*. As well as sugar, the ingenios produce molasses for making rum and alcohol, and the waste is used for feeding cattle. Most of the sugar produced around Tucumán and in the provinces of Salta and Jujuy is eaten by the Argentines themselves.

In the subtropical region of Argentina's north-east, rice and cotton are grown. Cotton was first grown in the Chaco area early in the twentieth century, and took over huge areas. Production was at a peak in the 1950s, but now the growers have to compete with cheaper production from other countries, and less cotton is grown. The British also introduced tea in Misiones. Although this is sold in Argentina, most of it is exported, as the Argentines prefer to drink a herb tea called *maté*. Maté is also grown in the north of the country, on the borders with Paraguay. The yerba maté tree grows naturally in the jungles there, reaching heights of up to 15 metres (50 feet), although when cultivated it is kept to three or four metres high (10 to 13 feet). The leaves are picked, dried and brewed in the same way as tea, and then the liquid is drunk from a gourd or wooden jar through a metal straw. Tobacco is another tropical crop produced in the region of Mesopotamia and the north-west of Argentina. It is sold to a state company which is in charge of all the cigarette production in the country. The heat of north-eastern Argentina is also ideal for the production of fruit such as oranges, lemons and grapefruit, and Argentina grows its own bananas in the northern provinces of Salta and Formosa.

Wines in the Andes

It was the Jesuits, among the first Spanish settlers, who brought vines from Europe to Argentina four centuries ago. They planted them in the west of the country, where the soils of the foothills of the Andes, plus the sun and water from rainfall and the mountain rivers meant that the vines could thrive. Now Mendoza and San Juan, two provinces in the west of Argentina, produce 20 million hectolitres of wine each year, making Argentina the world's largest producer of wine outside Europe. Most of this is red wine, and is table wine rather than wine of a high quality. Some of the estates are trying to improve the quality of

Rivers which in spring are full of water from the melted snows of the Andes help irrigate the vineyards in La Rioja. First brought here by Spanish monks in the sixteenth century, vines are now grown in over 2000 vineyards in Argentina.

their wines, and there is one well-known variety named after the Aberdeen Angus. The wine is grown on large estates, not the small traditional vineyards as in France. Many thousands of seasonal workers from the western provinces of Argentina, as well as a large number of Chileans from across the Andes, help in the wine harvest from February to April, and there are many celebrations of the wine harvest. The bulk of the wine is sold in Argentina itself, since most people drink wine with their meal every evening. About half of the wine exported goes to the Soviet Union.

Fruit, vegetables and fish
Mendoza is increasingly becoming a centre for fruit and vegetables, which are sent by lorry to the markets on the east coast. Further south, 120 000 tonnes of apples are grown each year in the protected valleys of the Río Negro in Patagonia. Most of this production is exported to Europe.

Although Argentina has over 2500 kilometres (1500 miles) of Atlantic coast, the enormous Río de la Plata estuary and many other large rivers and lakes, its fishing industry is not very developed. This is mainly because the Argentines prefer to eat beef rather than fish. They eat an average of five kilos or 12 pounds of fish per year, 20 times less than the average amount of meat they consume. One of the main centres for sea fishing is the port of Mar del Plata, where shellfish are caught for the summer tourists, and deep sea fishing is practised in the winter months. Altogether, about 400 000 tonnes of sea and freshwater fish are caught in Argentina each year.

5

From corned beef to cars

For much of its history, Argentina has made and sold products closely linked to its agriculture. When it was a Spanish colony, leather, wheat and mules were sent over the Andes mountains to Peru, which was a much more important country for the Spaniards. Towns in the north of Argentina close to Peru like Salta and Córdoba were larger than the port of Buenos Aires, as all trade with Spain was supposed to be carried out via Lima, the main port of Peru. Goods from Spain were also brought in overland from the north, and the colony was not allowed to trade

All Argentina's ports have large slaughterhouses. Cattle and other animals are brought here by road and rail, killed, and the meat chilled ready for export.

with other countries. However, by the end of the eighteenth century, Buenos Aires had become a centre for goods smuggled in from European countries other than Spain, especially Britain. These varied from textiles from Manchester to many thousands of black slaves, who were brought across from the port of Montevideo in Uruguay.

After independence in the nineteenth century, Buenos Aires and the other ports of the east coast sold Argentina's growing number of agricultural products and brought in factory-made goods from Britain, France and Germany. One writer in the mid-nineteenth century complained that a typical Argentine gaucho on the pampas wore a woollen poncho made in England, carried an English knife, cooked in English pots and pans and rode on a saddle imported from France. The only Argentine thing he had was his horse.

The start of industry

This pattern of selling meat and cereals abroad and using the money earned to import manufactured goods was the basis of Argentine trade for many years. The first industries were those connected with exporting food and animal skins: the *saladeros* where meat was salted before it was shipped abroad, leather tanneries, wool-dyeing mills, small factories for processing food and workshops to repair ships. Most of these industries were based near the ports, on the eastern side of the country. They offered ready work, and so the majority of the new immigrants stayed and worked there rather than moving inland to become farmers. On the land, most of

The dairy industry
There has traditionally been a strong industry based around milk and milk products in Argentina. There are some 3 500 000 dairy cows, which give 5 billion litres of milk per year. Nine hundred dairy factories turn this into butter, yoghurt and excellent cheeses like Mar del Plata (similar to the Dutch cheese Edam) or Chubut (like Cheddar cheese). The factories also produce milk sweets such as *dulce de leche,* a kind of soft fudge that is a national delicacy, and rich chocolate biscuits known as *alfajores.*

the work was for a few months only. Many agricultural labourers worked on the crop, sugar or wine harvests for a few months, then went to the towns to look for work there.

As the new immigrants increased in number, these towns grew rapidly in size. This in turn created the need for industries which would supply the clothing, food and the other necessities of life the immigrants wanted. When it became hard to buy these things in Europe because of the First World War, or the Great Depression in 1929, people in Argentina started making them for themselves. During the Second World War, from 1939 to 1945, there was even less chance to import goods made in Europe or the United States. When General Perón came to power after the war, he encouraged the Argentines to make their own goods, and the industries producing things like cars, iron and steel, and household items such as radios, refrigerators or washing machines quickly expanded. Once again, they were based mainly in

Buenos Aires and the other large towns on the Río de la Plata estuary, where there were plenty of people to work in the new factories and to buy the new products. The wealth of the rest of the country was still based almost entirely on agriculture.

Mining

Mining is the only industry that is not centred around the east of the country, but is carried out mostly in the Andes mountain areas and in remote parts of Patagonia. Argentina has very rich mineral resources, but these have not yet been fully exploited. Only 30 per cent of Argentina has been properly surveyed by geologists to see what minerals it might contain. Most of the 16 or so metals mined are found in the Andean provinces. Jujuy in the far north of Argentina accounts for 75 per cent of the total mineral production. Some of the mines are high in the mountains. For example, El Aguilar, owned by a United States company, extracts zinc, lead and silver in a mine at over 4500 metres (15 000 feet) which employs 5000 miners.

Iron is also mined in Jujuy at Zapla, and since the 1960s deposits found in the southern province of Río Negro have supplied half Argentina's needs for this metal. Other non-metallic minerals are also mined, the most important being salt from the salt beds in the Andean foothills, clay and kaolin in the province of Buenos Aires, and sulphur in Salta. There are known to be several large coal deposits throughout the country, but the only ones worked are at Río Turbio, in the southern province of Santa Cruz. Here a town of 15 000 people has grown up around the mines, which

Argentina has large deposits of coal but most of it is not easy to use. Only in Patagonia are there any coal mines such as this one at Rio Turbio.

have been working since the end of the Second World War. Most of Argentina's coal is not easy or cheap to mine because, for one thing, it is cheaper to bring coal all the way from Poland for Argentina's power stations. However, there are thought to be coal reserves of some 600 million tonnes, which could be an important reserve of fuel in the future.

All kinds of energy

Argentina has produced all the oil it needs since the early 1980s. The first discovery of oil was made at Comodoro Rivadavia in 1907 when engineers were drilling for water. Production now is 26 000 000 cubic metres (917 800 000 cubic feet) per year, and comes mainly from the provinces of

This new oil refinery is at the extreme south of Argentina. It is part of a complex of oil wells and refineries that help keep Argentina self-sufficient in oil supplies.

Mendoza, Santa Cruz and Chubut. Most of it is sent by pipeline to Buenos Aires and other cities, where there are refineries and new petro-chemical industries which transform the oil into fuels, plastics and other products. Another important way of producing energy is by using the power of the rivers from the Andes or in the north-east of Argentina. A huge dam is being built on the border with Paraguay at Yacireta, as Argentina continues to build up its hydro-electric power system. Argentina also has two nuclear power stations at Atucha in the province of Buenos Aires and Embalse Río Tercero in Córdoba. There are plans to open a third in the near future, as the country is rich in the natural uranium used to make this kind of energy. Studies have also been made to see if it would be worthwhile to use the power of the winds which sweep across Patagonia almost all the time. Only small projects have been tried so far, but there is a large potential for the future in this clean, constantly available form of energy.

Small factories and workshops

About one in five people in Argentina now work in industry, more than are employed in agriculture. Most of the factories are concentrated in the estuary of the Río de la Plata. Almost 50 per cent of all Argentina's industry is within 50 miles of the capital Buenos Aires. There are few large factories and most Argentines work in small plants with less than 100 workers. About 25 per cent work in the food, drinks and tobacco industry, while another 25 per cent are employed in making iron and steel and cars. The largest factory is the steelworks at San Nicolás in the province of Buenos Aires. This provides the iron and steel for the country's heavy industries, including the car factories which are mostly based at Córdoba, a large city about 800 kilometres (500 miles) north-west of the capital. Although Argentina produced its own makes of cars in the 1950s, foreign companies such as Ford, Volkswagen or Renault now have factories in Argentina to assemble their models. Córdoba is also the centre for railway manufacturing, and for

Argentina's aircraft industry. The other main heavy industry is shipbuilding, which is very important as nearly all Argentina's foreign trade is by boat. There are large shipyards at Tigre in the delta of the Río de la Plata, and at Río Santiago.

Trading with the world

Most of Argentina's trade is still with the United States and Europe. In the last 100 years, it has preferred to ship its goods to these countries rather than to send them by land to other countries in Latin America. This is because the Latin American nations produced similar things, had less money to buy Argentine goods, and could not sell manufactured goods back to Argentina.

Buenos Aires is the largest port in Latin America, and one of the busiest in the world, exporting everything from cereals and cars to minerals. Other ports deal mostly with

The port of Buenos Aires
The docks at Buenos Aires are the liveliest place in Argentina. Nearly 60 per cent of everything sold abroad passes through here, and 90 per cent of all the goods brought into the country are unloaded in one of the docks at Riachuelo, Dock Sur, Puerto Madero or Puerto Nuevo. Buenos Aires is not an ideal harbour, however, the Río de la Plata is only eight metres (30 feet) deep here, and because it constantly brings down sand and gravel from the north, the port has to be dredged all the time to stop it silting up. There are plans to build a new deepwater port further out towards the Atlantic at Punta Medanos, but nothing has so far come of them.

Modern trucks and cranes help shift ore in the port of Buenos Aires. The port deals with everything from minerals to cars, and is by far the largest in Argentina, although the Río de la Plata is constantly silting up with soil and sand.

agricultural exports, like Rosario further up the Río de la Plata, or Bahía Blanca in the south. Boats also travel upriver from Rosario to Mesopotamia and Paraguay, to bring down the subtropical produce and timber from those regions. Argentina is now trying to sell more of the goods it makes to neighbouring countries in Latin America, and this trade in the region is likely to become more important in the years to come.

6 Transport in Argentina

Argentina is so large that communications inside it have often been a problem. Until recently, much of Patagonia and the north-eastern provinces have been cut off from the rest of the country. Argentina also has difficult natural boundaries with its neighbours, which made contact with them difficult before air travel became common. It is also a long way by sea and air from Europe and the United States, so its links with these centres are not easy.

Mules and railways
When Argentina was a Spanish colony, most of the trade was carried by mules and horse-drawn carts along rough tracks. The longest journeys then were up through Bolivia to Peru, from where Argentina was governed. The towns of the interior had little contact with Buenos Aires, which was then a small port on the estuary of the Río de la Plata. This situation changed dramatically about 120 years ago. Around this time, British companies went to Argentina to build railways in order to bring the meat from the pampas to the port of Buenos Aires. Though the first railway in Argentina was built in 1857, it was between 1880 and 1906 that the system grew enormously, from 2500 to 20 000 kilometres (1500 to 12 500 miles). Buenos Aires was the centre of all these lines, and different stations were constructed in the capital to serve different parts of the country. Local stations

along the various lines were built exactly like those in Britain, and even today it is not unusual to see equipment on the railways that was made in Britain. Many of the villages on the pampas grew up around these railway stations. At its height, with 46 000 kilometres (28 000 miles) of track, Argentina had the sixth largest railway system in the world.

Railways are still essential for linking the main towns of Argentina, although in general the long-distance buses are quicker and now take 80 per cent of passengers. A train journey from Buenos Aires to Jujuy in the north of the country takes over a day. Steam trains are used in the Andes mountains, where the locomotives have to climb to more than 4000 metres (13 000 feet). Two spectacular journeys link Argentina with the north

The railway that links Argentina and Chile climbs over some high mountain passes. In this pass the railway is protected from rockfalls and snow drifts by long tunnels.

of Chile between Salta and Antofagasta, and Bolivia via Jujuy and La Quiaca. The railways never reached the far south of Argentina, because of the bad weather conditions, and now end at Bariloche. There have been attempts recently to modernize the railway network, but it is still losing passengers and goods to the roads. One problem left over from the days of rapid growth of the system is the fact that there are three different gauges, or distances between the rails, in the tracks, which makes it impossible to run one kind of train throughout Argentina.

Roads, tunnels and bridges

Argentina's road system grew rapidly in the twentieth century. It was in the 1950s that it began to compete with the railways for passengers and goods, and now carries 90 per cent of goods and an even higher percentage of all the passenger journeys. Most of the national highways start from Buenos Aires, and sometimes the connections overland, for example between Mendoza in the west and Tucumán in the north-west, are still difficult. This is particularly true in Patagonia, where the communications between east and west regions are almost non-existent. Of about 140 000 kilometres (87 000 miles) of road, only 30 per cent are properly made up. The rest are dirt roads that are often blocked by rain or floods.

Road links between Argentina and its westerly neighbour Chile have been greatly improved since the opening in the early 1980s of the tunnel through the Andes near Mendoza. More recently still, the Colon to Paysandú and Gualeguaychú to Fray Bentos bridges were opened between

Argentina and Uruguay. These have greatly increased trade by truck between the two countries where before all goods and passengers had to be transported across the estuary of the Río de la Plata, a distance of at least 40 kilometres (25 miles). Many Argentines who visit Uruguay as tourists still take ferries or hydrofoils across the water. Another attraction for tourists in Argentina is the Pan-American highway, which runs 5200 kilometres (3230 miles) from La Quiaca in the

This is the southern tip of Argentina at Ushuaia. As the signposts show, it is over 5000 kilometres from here to Argentina's northern border with Bolivia at La Quiaca. Buenos Aires, the capital, is about halfway up the mainland part of the country.

north to Ushuaia in the south of Tierra del Fuego.

In the countryside of Argentina, horses are still very common as a means of transport, and all Argentines pride themselves on being good horse riders.

River boats and sea cruises

The Río de la Plata continues upstream in the Paraná and Uruguay rivers for about 3000 kilometres (2200 miles). Since the days of the Spaniards, boats have been used to transport fruit, timber and the other products of the north-east down to the capital, and to take passengers to and fro. Only in the past 25 years, with so many more cars and trucks in Argentina, and the building of tunnels under the major rivers, has this river traffic lessened.

Earlier this century, the only way from Argentina to Europe or the United States was by ship. The trip could take anything up to three weeks. Liners travelled regularly between Buenos Aires, New York, England, Spain and Italy. Now very few of these ships remain, as most people prefer the rapid journey by plane.

Today's airlines

Internal airways are very important in Argentina because of the great distances. It takes two hours to fly from Buenos Aires west to Mendoza, the same time as from London to Madrid, and three hours from Buenos Aires to the far south, as long as the journey from New York to Texas. The Austral airline covers the different regions, and there are airports in nearly all the provincial capitals. Buenos Aires has two airports, one for

Air travel is important in Argentina as the distances between towns are so great. These businessmen have arrived at Concordia Airport in a Fokker, which is a popular plane in Argentina.

international flights at Ezeiza 15 kilometres (nine miles) outside the city, and one inside the city known as the Aeroparque Jorge Newbery. This handles internal flights and ones across the Río de la Plata estuary to Uruguay and Brazil. There are regular flights to Argentina from most of the larger European countries and from the United States. The flight from Europe takes between 12 to 16 hours. The Argentines themselves are keen travellers, and those who can afford it visit Europe or the United States in their winter months of July and August. The Argentine national airline is called Aerolineas Argentinas, and flies to many European and Latin American countries as well as to the United States.

Cars and buses

There are over three million private cars in Argentina. Even today, there are often not enough new cars to meet demand, and people try to win them in a lottery so that they will not have to wait so long. Most of the big European manufacturers, apart from the British, sell cars in Argentina, and there are also many United States and Japanese models. New motorways were built in the 1970s to cope with the traffic, but there are often jams in the centre of Buenos Aires and in most other big cities. Traffic in the towns is helped by the fact that they are designed on a chessboard system, with roads parallel and at right angles to each other. Many people prefer to travel to work on buses. The buses are privately run, and the brightly-coloured buses known as *colectivos* are a typical sight in city streets. There are also many of the characteristic black and yellow taxis. Buenos Aires also has a small underground railway system connecting the city centre with the suburbs.

Colectivos

Colectivos are the typical single-decker buses of Buenos Aires and the other big towns of Argentina. They are powerful Mercedes buses first introduced 40 years ago. The driver often decorates his bus with painted scrolls, verses, oraments or other decorations. As in all Latin America, youngsters selling cheap goods often board the colectivos and try to persuade the passengers to buy from them.

7   Argentina today

As it is so large, Argentina can grow all kinds of fruit and vegetables, from subtropical crops like oranges and bananas to potatoes, apples, and pears. This produce is brought quickly to the large cities and towns, where corner shops and markets put on vivid displays.

There are now about 31 million Argentines, more than half of them living in big cities. Buenos Aires, with 11 million inhabitants, is by far the largest city, but a million people live in Córdoba, Santa Fe and Rosario, while half a million people live in La Plata in the two largest towns of the interior, Mendoza and Tucumán. Many people work in factories, but there are also great numbers, especially women, who work in offices for the government. A high proportion of the families where the parents work have a maid to look after the children and help with the cooking and shopping. These domestics come from the provinces of the interior or from Paraguay and Uruguay.

Flats and houses

Blocks of flats have mostly replaced houses in the centre of the big cities. The typical *barrio* or local neighbourhood of Buenos Aires and other towns consists of a central square with a monument to an Argentine hero in the middle, and a church and the town hall along two sides of it. The main shopping street usually contains a city market where meat, fruit and vegetables can be bought. Other food shops will include a baker's, offering a wide range of bread and pasteries, a pizzeria and an ice-cream parlour. There is often a cafe on the corner of the street, as many Argentines love to sit out, drink coffee and chat with friends as they watch the world go by. Each neighbourhood also has a cinema, often rather run-down these days, though there is still a large public for films.

However, most of the rich cities are surrounded by poor slums or *villas miserias*. The people live in shacks without electricity or running water. No government has built enough proper houses for all the people who come to the cities.

There are often slums on the outskirts of Argentina's big cities. People make their shacks from pieces of wood, tins, or whatever else they can find to build with.

Cosmopolitan Buenos Aires

Buenos Aires, the Argentine capital, is a huge city of 11 million people from many different backgrounds. A local joke says that an inhabitant of the city, known as a 'porteño' because Buenos Aires is a port, 'speaks Spanish, eats Italian, dresses like a Frenchman, and thinks he is an Englishman.' The city itself looks very European, with buildings in French, Italian and British styles. There are German, Jewish, Chinese and Japanese restaurants as well as many Italian and Spanish places. Buenos Aires also attracts thousands of people from the Argentine provinces, who come in search of work. Many thousands more come from the neighbouring countries of Paraguay, Bolivia or Uruguay, also in the hope of finding work.

Italian immigrants first settled in the Boca district in the port of Buenos Aires. Many of the wooden houses are painted in bright colours, and there is a strong sense of identity. The people there often still speak Italian in the streets.

The working day

Because the weather is often very hot, many Argentines break their working day. They start early, at eight am, and work until mid-day. They then eat lunch and often have an afternoon nap or siesta before going back to work at three pm. This means they do not finish until seven pm, so that social life such as the theatre, the cinema or music has to begin later than in many other countries. Cafes and restaurants stay open until very late, as Argentines are accustomed to go there after they have been out to their evening's entertainment. In recent years, because of the difficult economic situation, increasing numbers of people have more than one job and have to work many hours.

The Argentines have inherited the tradition of cafes from Spain and Italy. They like to have breakfast there, or morning coffee, and will lunch on a snack in a corner cafe. In the evening, they go there for drinks with friends.

Religion

Sunday is a day for religion and sport. Argentina is a Catholic country. The president and vice-president of the nation must be Catholics, and almost 90 per cent of Argentines are officially Catholic. For many, this does not go beyond visits to the church for weddings, funerals and pilgrimages on big festival days. The most popular place for pilgrimage is at Luján, 50 kilometres (30 miles) outside Buenos Aires. Every year, tens of thousands of people make the trip on foot to celebrate the virgin in the cathedral there. The Catholic Church itself has often been very politically conservative and does not welcome change. It was not until 1987 that President Alfonsín managed to have divorce made legal in Argentina, against strong opposition from the Catholic bishops.

Buenos Aires is the city with the second largest Jewish population in the Americas after New York. Several of its neighbourhoods are full of Jewish people who observe their own religion and customs strictly, and speak Yiddish or Hebrew. The other main religion is the Protestant Church, and there is an Anglican bishop of Buenos Aires as well as a Catholic one. Many of the smaller groups who came to live in Argentina practise their own religions freely. All children born in Argentina though must have Christian names, and this sometimes causes problems for the immigrant groups.

The *asado*

At Sunday lunch-time, everyone who can leaves the large towns to eat an *asado*. This is a barbecue of many different kinds of beef cooked in the open air. Richer familes will go to a *quinta*, or weekend place outside the town. Many others are members of social clubs where they can eat and play sport. A very popular place for this close to Buenos Aires is Tigre, at the delta of the Río de la Plata. Here there are hundreds of small islands which can be reached by motor boat, and people either have weekend cottages or go to clubs organized by the trade unions or sporting associations. Those who have to stay in town get together with relatives and friends.

Life in the interior
Fewer than 50 per cent of the Argentine people live in the interior away from the Atlantic sea coast. In Patagonia for example, there are far more sheep than people. According to the 1980 census, there were only 115 000 people living in the southern province of Santa Cruz, less than one person per square kilometre. It is only in these remote regions that the original inhabitants of Argentina are still to be found. Altogether, they make up less than one per cent of the total population. They live in small groups, and work at farming to survive. The remaining 40 000 or so original peoples, the Araucanos or Mapuche, live in the foothills of the Andes in the south, preserving some of their traditions. In the Chaco region of the north-east, a few Guaraní-speaking groups lead the nomadic hunting lives that their ancestors had thousands of years ago. Most of them though have been persuaded to settle and farm by Christian missionaries.

In the north-western Andean provinces of Salta

Many markets are held on the hillsides of the Andean mountains in north Argentina. Here, the local people buy and sell food, clothes, pottery, and handicrafts.

and Jujuy there are also groups of the Colla people. They have mostly come down from Bolivia, and also lead lives farming for their own needs. They live in simple houses made of a mixture of clay and straw called *adobe*. They have kept some of their customs and beliefs, and though they often also worship in Catholic churches, their cult is to the Earth, the sun and the moon. Their traditional medicine based on herbs is still practised in some places, but mostly they are integrated into the way of life of the rest of Argentina.

Land of the Ches

In the rest of Latin America, Argentina is often known as the 'land of the ches'. This is because when they speak Argentines often add the word 'che', as in the phrases: 'How are you, che?' or 'Che can you help?' The word 'che' comes from the Mapuche language and means 'man', so its use is like that of the word 'man' in the United States. That is how Ernesto Guevara, an Argentine doctor who helped to make the revolution in Cuba and fought throughout Latin America to extend it there, became known as 'Che' Guevara. The Spanish of Argentina is quite different from that of Spain. It is pronounced like Italian because of the many Italian immigrants, and there are a lot of Italian words mixed in. Buenos Aires has its own slang, known as *lunfardo,* which is also thought to have come from Italy. In lunfardo, 'pibe' and 'piba' are 'boy' and 'girl', 'morfi' is 'food'.

Life on an estancia

Much of the interior of Argentina is taken up by huge ranches or *estancias*. These often consist of a large main house, where the owners and the manager live. The owners usually spend much of the time in the city, and it is common for them to fly out to their ranches at weekends. There are also houses for the cowboys or gauchos who do all the work on these cattle estates. The other agricultural estates employ few people nowadays, as the work is mostly done by machine, though the grape and sugar harvests attract large numbers of seasonal labourers. The towns of the interior tend to be small and to be based around agriculture. The people are usually descended from the Spanish settlers in origin. They tend to feel that they, and not the inhabitants of Buenos Aires, are the real Argentines, and there is a lot of rivalry between the two groups.

Health and welfare

Argentina has one of the most developed health systems in Latin America. There are few problems of people suffering from malnutrition, when people get too little food to eat, as meat and other food is usually very cheap. However, the recent high inflation has brought problems for some of the poorer people in the towns. The climate is not bad enough to cause health problems, though in the interior a disease known as *mal de chagas*, which is carried by insects and can infect the blood and kill people, has always been a major problem. Buenos Aires and the other main cities have modern hospitals, and there are clinics and small hospitals throughout the country.

Argentina has a reputation throughout Latin America for its excellently trained doctors and nurses. The ratio of doctors and nurses to the rest of the population is almost the same as in most European countries. The number of children who die at birth or in the first year is also as low as that in many countries in Western Europe. Though medical treatment from a doctor is not free, most people are insured through their work, with the trade union paying almost all the cost of the employee's insurance. Anyone who does not have insurance can go to a public hospital for attention. In the interior, a system of ambulances links the remote areas with clinics and hospitals in the towns.

Young Argentina

Unlike other countries in Latin America, Argentina does not have a rapidly increasing population. In 1985, only about 15 per cent of Argentines were under 16. Children start school at the age of six, and are meant to attend until they are at least 14, though in many rural areas a large number of children leave school earlier to start work and help the family income. It was President Sarmiento who set up the public school system over 100 years ago, since he believed that 'to govern is to educate'. State education is free and non-religious, but parents who wish their children to follow a particular faith can send them to special schools. Education is seen as an important way of bringing such a large country together, so schoolchildren are taught the same subjects from the far north in Jujuy to Tierra del Fuego in the south.

Most children in Argentina are well fed and healthy. There is not a rapidly growing population, so there are good health and education facilities for the children.

Children either attend school from 8 am to midday, or go in the afternoon. Each day starts with the raising of the national flag and the singing of the Argentine anthem. The range of subjects taught is similar to that in Europe or the United States, with mathematics, sciences, Argentine history and geography to the fore. The main foreign language studied is English, although some schools teach French. The school system is like the French or that followed in the United States, with the children having to pass from one grade to the next by getting a good enough mark in each subject.

Young Argentines have a good education based on a system similar to that in France or the United States. However, after leaving school, many of them want to leave Argentina as they feel they will have better jobs in Europe or the United States.

At the end of primary schooling, pupils can go to a *colegio,* where they study academic subjects which lead to an exam called the *bachillerato,* at the end of secondary school. Alternatively, students can go to more vocational schools, where they are trained in specific trades or occupations.

Schoolchildren can also choose to become teachers themselves, and then they go to an *escuela normal*, where teachers are trained.

If a student is successful in the bachillerato exam, he or she has the right to go to one of Argentina's universities. Almost half a million Argentines study full or part-time at one of the country's 50 universities, but most of them continue to live at home, as there are few grants to pay for studies. Many students work to finance their way through college. The first university in Argentina was founded by the Spaniards at Córdoba in the seventeenth century. This and most of the others are public and independent, but there are Catholic universities and private ones as well.

Young men in Argentina all have to do national service in one of the armed forces. There have been many protests about this, especially since the 1976 military government, when the recruits were used to capture and imprison opponents of the regime, and after the war on the Falkland Islands, when young recruits were sent to fight professional British soldiers.

As the twenty-first century approaches, Argentina is facing a serious problem because many of its young people want to leave the country. They think they will find better jobs and have a more secure future in the United States or Europe.

8 Life outside work

For many years, most Argentines have enjoyed a high standard of living. Food has been cheap and plentiful, and earnings have left plenty of time for sport and cultural activities, though rising inflation is now causing problems. The mixture of different traditions brought by the immigrants and the native inhabitants has created a rich variety of cultural life. The good climate in the central area of the country also encouraged people to play outdoor games, and Argentina has a strong sporting tradition.

In 1986, Argentina won the coveted World Cup in Mexico City, led by their world famous captain, Diego Maradona.

Soccer

Soccer is the national game. Introduced by British sailors in the 1860s, and organized nationally by British immigrants in the 1890s, it has been

tremendously popular ever since. The professional teams play in two leagues and have a yearly national cup competition. Although every town has its own team, the best are based in Buenos Aires. The greatest rivals there are Boca Juniors, a team from the mainly Italian immigrant area of the port, and River Plate, nicknamed 'the millionaires', whose stadium is in a richer part of the city on the banks of the Río de la Plata estuary. Whenever these two teams play, crowds of 50 000 people or more go to watch. The national team has even more enthusiastic support. When it won the soccer World Cup in 1978 there were huge celebrations in the streets of Buenos Aires. These were repeated eight years later, when Maradona, their captain, who is often described as the world's best soccer player, led Argentina to victory in Mexico. It is sad but not uncommon that Maradona himself has often played football in Italy, where he is able to earn much more money than in Argentina.

Pato

Pato is a game played only in Argentina. Its name means 'a duck', as the poor animal was originally used as the ball. The game was for two teams of horsemen to grab the duck and ride back to their base with it. These games became so fierce, with a number of people even being killed, that in 1882 pato was banned. It was revived in 1938, this time with proper rules, and a leather ball with handles instead of a duck. The game is now played with two teams of four riders each, who have to get this ball through a basket at their opponents' end of the field.

Rugby was also brought to Argentina by the British, and is taught in many schools. The national team is known as The Pumas. It plays against other international sides, and has shown itself to be as good as the European teams. The third sport introduced by the British was cricket. This has never been as popular as the other two games, but is taught in the English-language schools and played by the Anglo-Argentine community in the suburbs of Buenos Aires.

Polo is a sport played by the rich in Argentina. Many of the world's best polo players and ponies come from here. The game is played by several thousand players throughout the country, who compete in Buenos Aires each year for the national championship.

Tennis, polo and motor racing

For many years, tennis was another sport played mostly by the rich. This situation changed in the 1960s when Argentine tennis players such as Guillermo Vilas had great success in international competitions. This made tennis very popular in

Argentina, and thousands of youngsters started to play. Many more clubs were opened in Buenos Aires and the other large towns. One of the most famous players to come out of this boom in popularity is Gabriela Sabatini, who reached the semi-finals of the Wimbledon tournament in 1986 when still only 16.

Polo is still very much a sport of the rich. Argentina has perfect conditions for this game played on horseback, as it has both flat, lush grass lawns for playing on, and a regular supply of trained ponies for riding. There are more than 6000 polo players registered in Argentina, and top professionals regularly travel to international competitions. In a country with such a tradition of fine horses, both horse racing and show jumping are popular too. Most towns have a horse-racing track where people can bet. The most important meetings are held at the San Isidro stadium in a Buenos Aires suburb.

Another kind of competition that is keenly watched is motor racing. Drivers such as Juan Fangio in the 1950s and Carlos Reutemann in the 1970s became national heroes when they won Grand Prix abroad, and the sport has a large television audience. Argentina used to hold a Grand Prix itself every year, but the instability in the country has meant this has had to be suspended.

Opera and cinema
Buenos Aires has a world-famous opera house, the Teatro Colón, and enjoys a strong tradition of European music, with several symphony orchestras and concert halls. Its theatre life is also

Buenos Aires has a lively and varied night life. This street in the centre of the city is full of cinemas.

very varied, and there are many cinemas, which receive North American, Italian and French films as well as those made in Argentina. Film-making enjoyed a boom in the 1980s when the democratic civilian government passed laws to encourage local directors, and some of these films like *Official Version* by Luis Puenzo have won the Argentine cinema an international reputation.

Music and books

Many Argentines love music. As well as the classical tradition of European music, they enjoy

The tango is Argentina's national dance. The man, who usually wears a suit and hat as in this photograph, leads the woman through a series of complicated steps.

their own tango music, which is Argentine jazz, and the country's folklore songs. These are usually sung by one person, to the accompaniment of a guitar, but music from the Andean region, played on a reed pipe and drums, is also very popular. In recent years, Argentine rock music, played by groups like Charly Garcia and Hemorrageo Cerebral has enjoyed great success not only in Argentina but in many other countries of Latin America as well.

Much music is played on the radio, which means that everyone can listen to it. There is a chain of national radio stations that covers the whole of Argentina, while many towns have several private radio stations. Colour television started in Argentina in 1976 when the football World Cup was held there. There are four television channels in Buenos Aires but, although about 60 per cent of all households have a television set, the quality of programmes is often not very high. Most Argentines prefer to read a daily newspaper to find out what is going on. There are half a dozen national daily papers, and many of the immigrant communities have one in their own language, like the *Buenos Aires Herald* or *Deutsches Tagesblatter*.

Argentines also have a great passion for books. For many years Argentina was a world centre for new and exciting books in Spanish. Argentine writers like Jorge Luis Borges and Julio Cortázar are world famous. Economic problems and political turmoil in the 1970s affected writers and the publishing industry badly, but there is still a great public demand for books. The national book fair held in Buenos Aires every year attracts as many as a million visitors. According to figures, only about five per cent of the population does not know how to read or write.

Summer and winter holidays

The weather in much of Argentina is very hot in January and February. Most Argentines try to get out of the cities for at least a few weeks. Every year, up to two million people flock to Mar del Plata and other resorts on the Atlantic coast between 400 and 500 kilometres (180 and 300 miles) from Buenos Aires. In many ways, they

Mar del Plata is a very popular seaside resort. The good climate allows Argentines plenty of opportunity for swimming and other seaside activities.

turn the seaside into another city, with shops, restaurants, and fashionable clothes on and off the beach. One of Mar del Plata's chief attractions is its casino, as many Argentines are keen roulette and poker players.

Winter holidays in July or August tend to be shorter. Recently, it has become fashionable to travel over 1000 kilometres (600 miles) south to ski in the Andes resort near Mendoza at Las Lenas or San Carlos de Bariloche. San Carlos is Argentina's main ski resort, about 1700 kilometres (980 miles) south-west of Buenos Aires. It was founded in 1895 by a German immigrant and looks very like an Alpine ski resort with chalets, pine trees and

Skiing is a fashionable sport among the wealthier Argentines. The season is during July and August, which is their winter.

cafés serving hot chocolate, a speciality of the town. Many Brazilians and Chileans also join the skiers there. Other Argentine city dwellers go to the hills in Córdoba to relax. Hill walking and mountain climbing are especially enjoyed by students.

9 Argentina's future

It is often said as a joke that 'Argentina is a country with a brilliant future behind it'. By this people mean that Argentina is very rich in many ways, yet the country never seems to fulfil the promise it has. For the future to be more rewarding, a lot of areas of the national life need to change. The country has a vast range of natural resources and does not have to import any oil or food. It has excellent opportunities for growth in agriculture and industry, and has a well-educated population that works and lives together without many social tensions. Argentina enjoys good relations with its neighbours, and apart from the recent clash with Britain over the Falkland Islands, it has enjoyed peace with the rest of the world for many years.

Since 1984, Argentina has again been governed by elected civilian politicians. It is important that this rule by president and parliament should continue through the coming years. In this way, Argentines who have lived through long periods of having military governments force laws upon them can learn that they should play an active part in running their own country. This will help build up more of a belief in the future of Argentina and the feeling that each person has something to contribute. The Peronist government under President Carlos Menem must make sure that the country is not divided, and that political stability brings benefits to everyone. Nobody wants a return to rule by the armed forces, but the politicians will have to show that they can bring real improvements if they are to stay in power.

Carlos Menem became president of Argentina in July 1989. As leader of the Peronist party, he has to unite all the Argentines to help them find a stable future as the country approaches the year 2000.

Though Argentina is rich, its people have become poorer over the past 30 years. Any government will have to make sure that the Argentines see their work rewarded. This means trying to find an answer to the problem of the debts which Argentina as a country owes to the banks in the rest of the world. At the same time, Argentina must hope that its exports of meat, fruit and other goods can earn more, while its local industries produce more.

New frontiers

Argentines also need to see their own country in a different way. President Alfonsín has suggested moving the capital of Argentina from Buenos Aires to Viedma, a small town 800 kilometres (500 miles) south in Patagonia. Nothing has come of this idea, but some change of this sort is needed to help stop the concentration of jobs, money and influence around Buenos Aires. The Peronist party now in power has strong support in the provinces, so it is planning to give more importance to provincial governments and to creating points for growth in Argentina's interior.

Argentina also needs to build up stronger links with the other countries of Latin America. A common market to help increase trade with Uruguay and Brazil is being set up. Much of the hope in Argentina's future seems to lie in looking for outlets for its goods and expertise among its neighbours.

Buenos Aires is a thriving modern city where high rise offices like these banks, house many businesses. If the government manages to sort out Argentina's inflation, the country has the potential for great development.

Index